BASIC STEPS TO DRUMMING

Drumming Made Easy

JEREMY YEO

To order additional copies of this book, contact
Toll Free +65 3165 7531 (Singapore)
Toll Free +60 3 3099 4412 (Malaysia)
www.partridgepublishing.com/singapore
orders.singapore@partridgepublishing.com

ISBN
978-1-5437-7073-5 (sc)
978-1-5437-7074-2 (e)

Print information available on the last page.

12/19/2022

PARTRIDGE

Table of Content

Introduction

1. Parts of a Drum Kit
2. Setting up your Drum Kit
3. Seating Posture
4. Warm-up Exercises
5. Types of Drumstick Grips
6. Drumming Terms
7. Music Chart Indications
8. Drum Notation

- The above stated are for both teachers and students to research on before commencing the use of this drumming book. You may easily find information online.

Note that all exercises are written in a 4/4 time signature in this book.

Every bar/measure holds 4 counts in crotchets.

Drum Kit

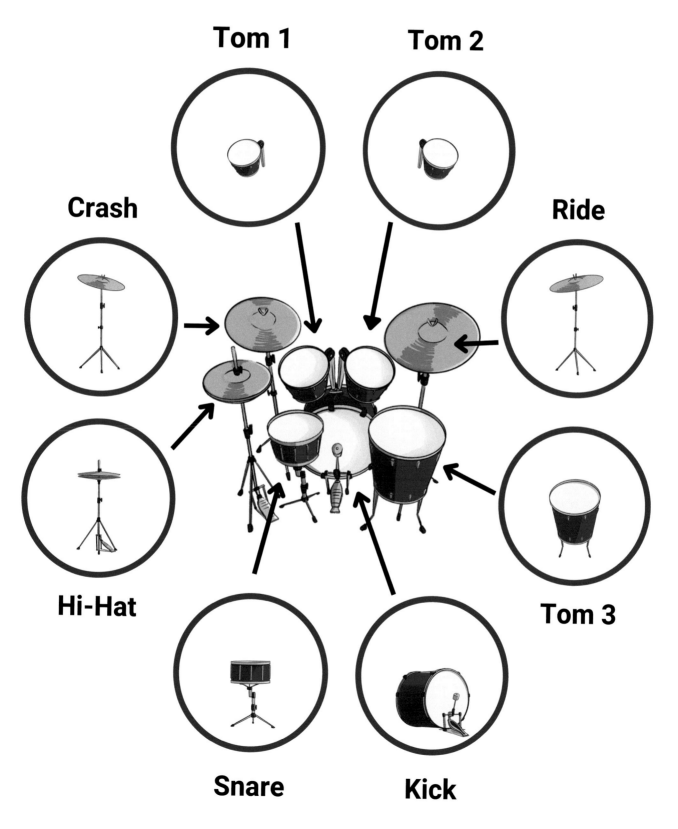

Tom 1

Tom 2

Crash

Ride

Hi-Hat

Tom 3

Snare

Kick

NOTE VALUE CHART

NOTES	RESTS

Whole Note / Semibreve

Half Note / Minim

Quarter Note / Crotchet

Eighth Note / Quaver

Sixteenth Note / Semiquaver

Quaver Note Triplet

Semiquaver Note Six-tuplet

INTRODUCTION

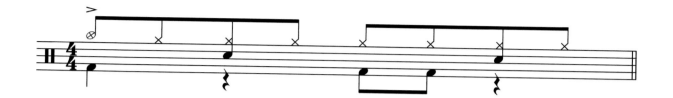

1. Parts of a Drum Kit

DRUMS
- Snare Drum
- Bass Drum / Kick Drum / Bass Kick
- Tom 1 / Left Tom / High Tom
- Tom 2 / Right Tom / Mid Tom
- Tom 3 / Floor Tom / Low Tom

CYMBALS
- Hi-Hat
- Crash Cymbal
- Ride Cymbal
- Splash Cymbal
- China Cymbal

2. Setting up your Drum Kit

3. Seating Posture

4. Warm-up Exercises

5. Types of Drumstick Grips
- French Grip
- German Grip
- American Grip
- Traditional Grip

6. Drumming Terms
- Sticking Pattern
- Rudiments
- Down Beat / Back Beat
- Accents / Ghost Notes (Grace Notes)
- Musical Pulse
- Dynamics

7. Music Chart Indications

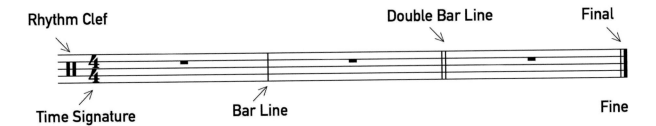

8. Drum Notation

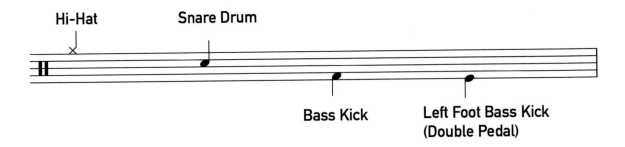

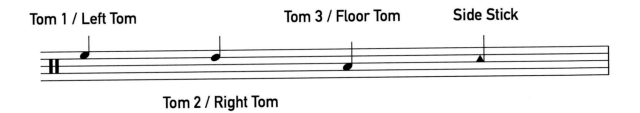

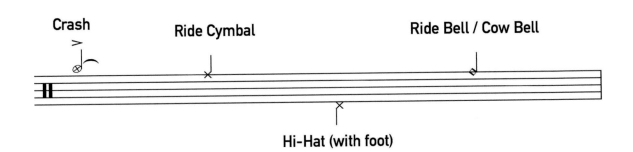

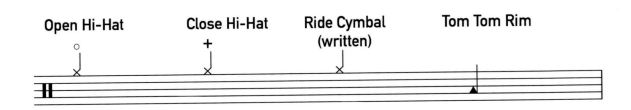

Simile Marks

Start Repeat

2 Bars Simile Marks

2

End Repeat

STICKING PATTERN INDICATIONS:

Right Hand - R

Left Hand - L

Kick Drum - K

LESSON 1: (1/4 Note)

9. Counting in 1/4 Notes

COUNT: 1 2 3 4

Hi - Hat

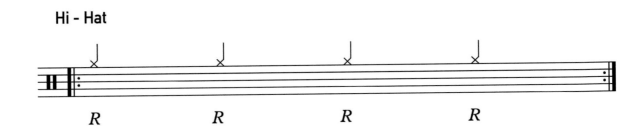

R   R   R   R

Snare Drum

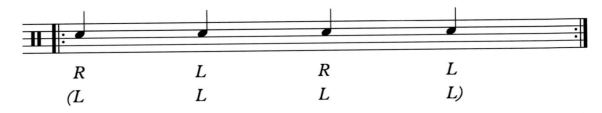

R   L   R   L
(L   L   L   L)

Bass Drum

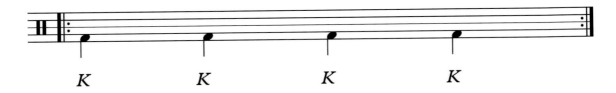

K   K   K   K

10. 1/4 Note Beat (Step by Step)

- Play these exercises replacing the Hi-Hat
with Ride Cymbal, Crash Cymbal, Floor Tom and Open Hi-Hat

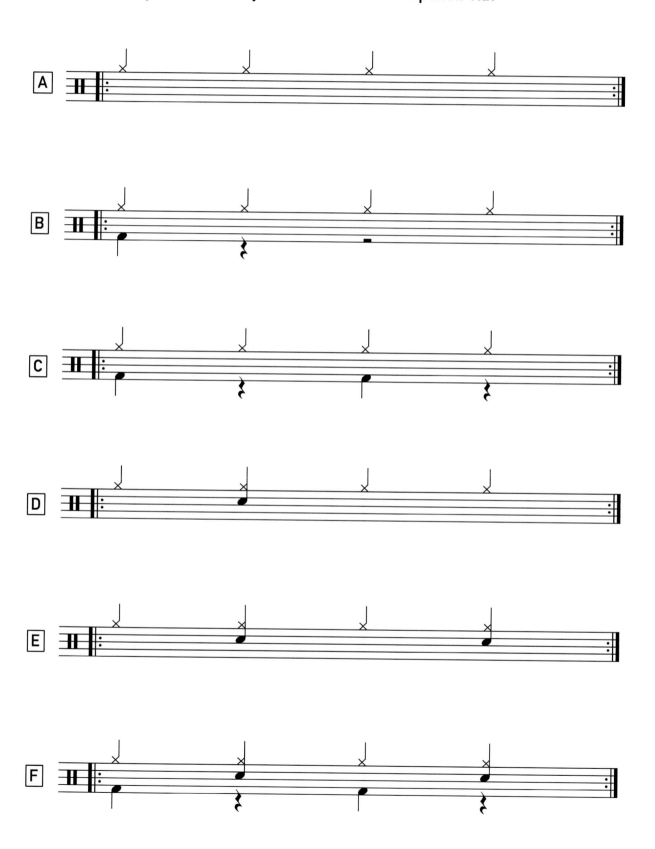

11. Rhythm + Fill-in Exercise

1 + 1

Fill-in on Snare Drum

Fill-in around the Drum Kit

12. Counting System 3 + 1

(1) **2 3 4**   - (Bar 1)

(2) **2 3 4**   - (Bar 2)

(3) **2 3 4**   - (Bar 3)

(4) **2 3 4**   - (Fill-in)

A̲ 3 bars of rhythm + 1 bar of Fill-in on Snare Drum

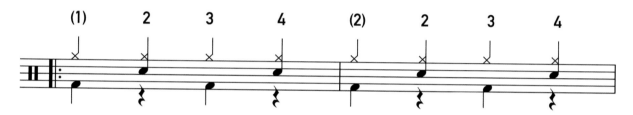

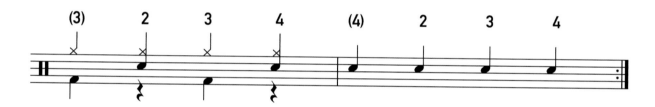

B̲ 3 bars of rhythm + 1 bar of Fill-in around the Drum Kit

13. 1/4 Note Rest

Alternate Sticking Pattern R L R L

16-bar Reading Exercise

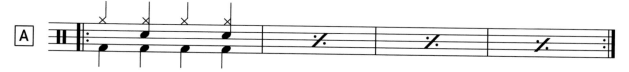

More 1/4 Note Rhythms

- Play these exercises replacing the Hi-Hat
with Ride Cymbal, Crash Cymbal, Floor Tom and Open Hi-Hat

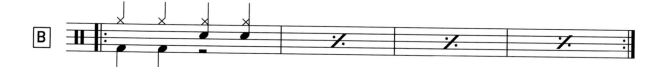

14. Crash Cymbal

LESSON 2: (1/8 Note)

15. Counting in 1/8 Notes

COUNT: 1 n 2 n 3 n 4 n

Hi - Hat

R R R R R R R R

Snare Drum

R L R L R L R L

Bass Drum

K K K K K K K K

Ride Cymbal (above the line)
(Ride)

Ride Cymbal (across the line)

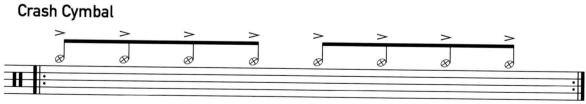

Crash Cymbal

16. 1/8 Note Beat (Step by Step)

- Play these exercises replacing the Hi-Hat
with Ride Cymbal, Crash Cymbal, Floor Tom and Open Hi-Hat

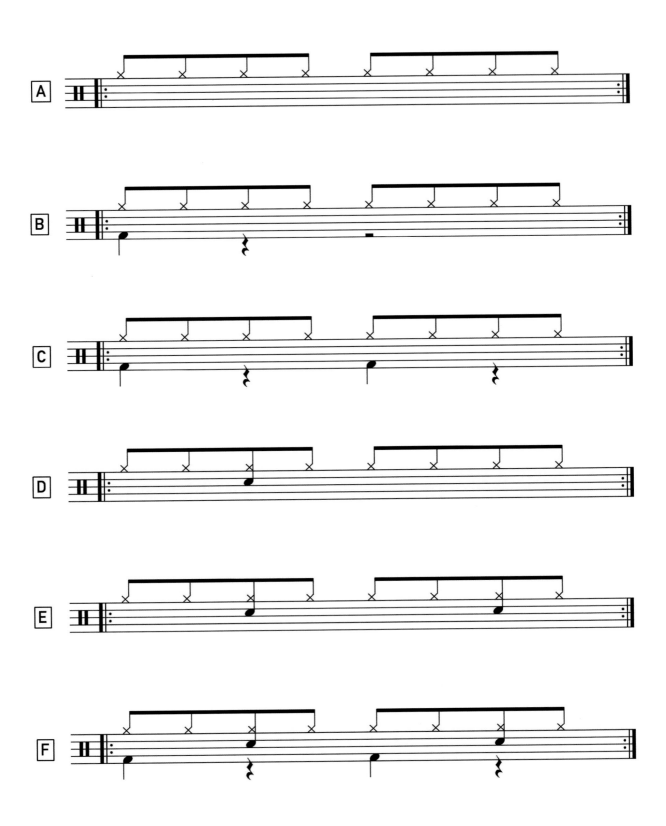

17. Rhythm + Fill-in Exercise

1 + 1

A Fill-in on Snare Drum

R L R L R L R L

B Fill-in around the Drum Kit

18. Counting System 3 + 1

(1) n 2 n 3 n 4 n   - (Bar 1)

(2) n 2 n 3 n 4 n   - (Bar 2)

(3) n 2 n 3 n 4 n   - (Bar 3)

(4) n 2 n 3 n 4 n   - (Bar 4)

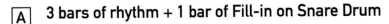

A 3 bars of rhythm + 1 bar of Fill-in on Snare Drum

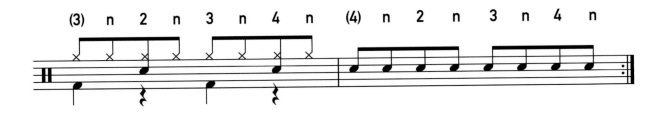

B 3 bars of rhythm + 1 bar of Fill-in around the Drum Kit

16

19. 1/8 Note Rest

A Hi-Hat

B Snare Drum

C Bass Drum

Ride Cymbal Bell

Linear Disco Beat

Stick Control Exercise - 1/4 and 1/8 note

A

B

C

D

8-bar Reading Exercise - 1/4 and 1/8 Notes

20. Rhythm Counting Styles

Counting in 1/4 and 1/8 Notes

Counting in 1/4 Notes

Counting in 1/8 Notes

1 n 2 n 3 n 4 n   1 n 2 n 3 n 4 n

C

21. Basic Rudiments

A Double Stroke

R   R   L   L   R   R   L   L

B Single Paradiddle (Mixed Sticking)

R   L   R   R   L   R   L   L

C Single Stroke + Double Stroke

R L R L R L R L   R R L L R R L L

D Single Stroke + Single Paradiddle

R L R L R L R L   R L R R L R L L

22. More Basic 1/8 Note Rhythms

- Play these exercises replacing the Hi-Hat
with Ride Cymbal, Crash Cymbal, Floor Tom and Open Hi-Hat

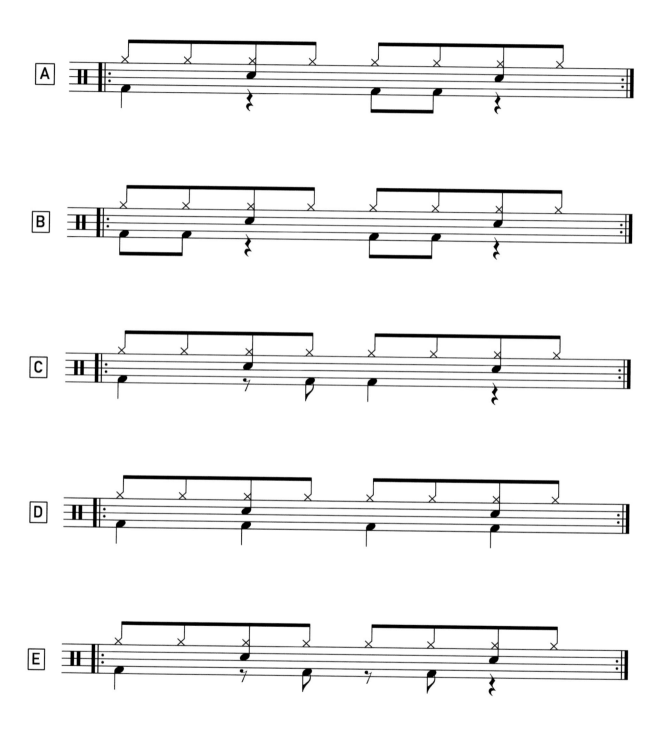

LESSON 3: (1/16 Note)

23. Counting in 1/16 Notes

COUNT: 1ena 2ena 3ena 4ena

2-bar Stick Control Exercise.

4-bar Stick Control Exercise.

24. Broken 1/16 Notes

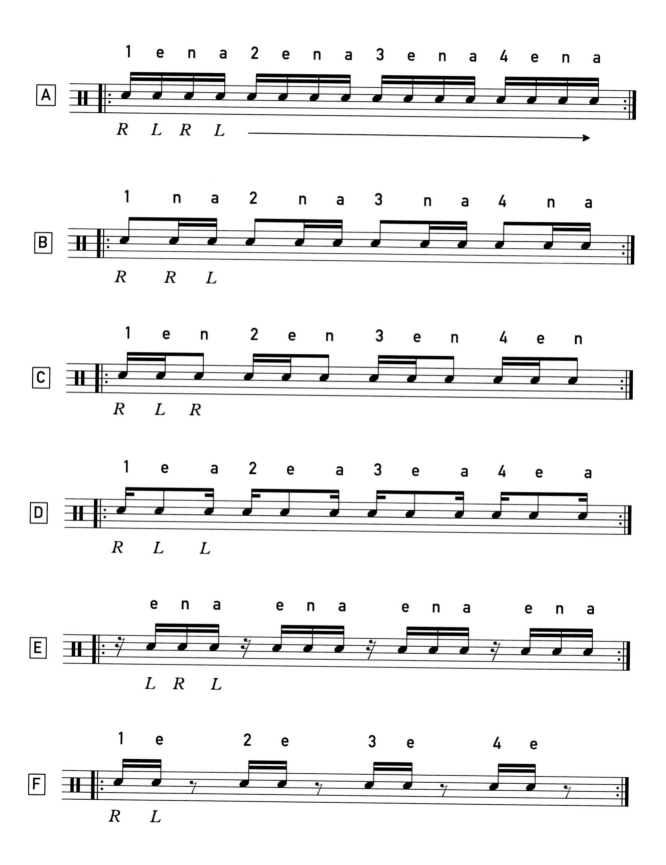

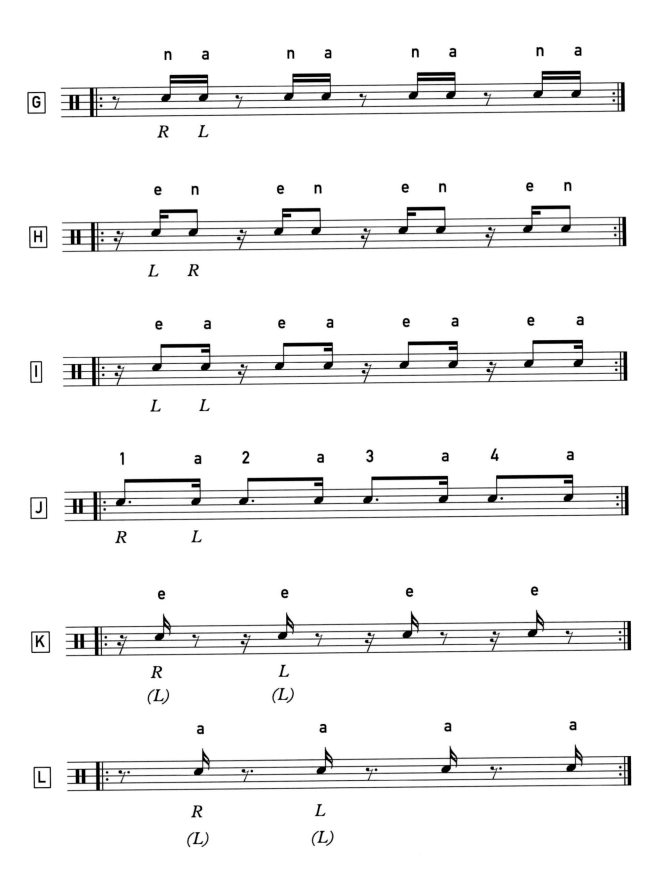

25. Broken 1/16 Notes around the Drum Set

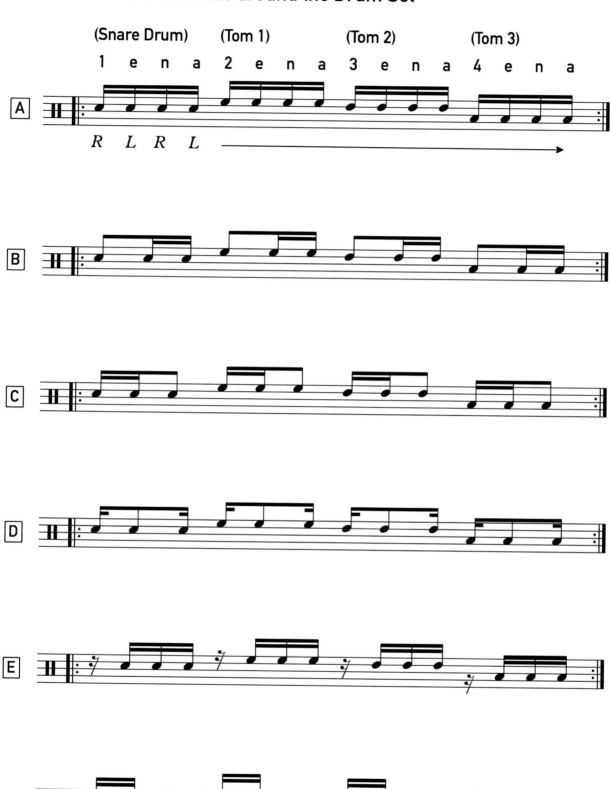

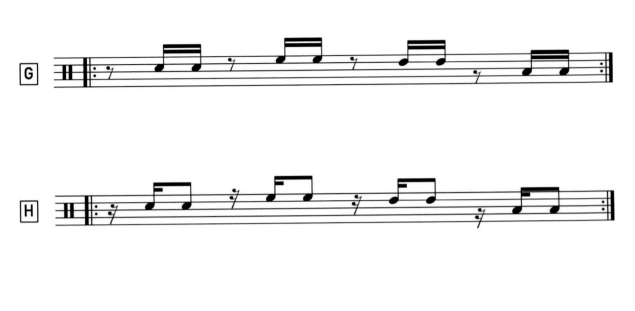

26

LESSON 4: (Accents and Ghost Notes)

(Loud)   (Soft)

26. 1/4 Note Accents

Sticking Patterns

1) R - L - R - L   2) L - R - L - R

3) R - R - R - R   4) L - L - L - L

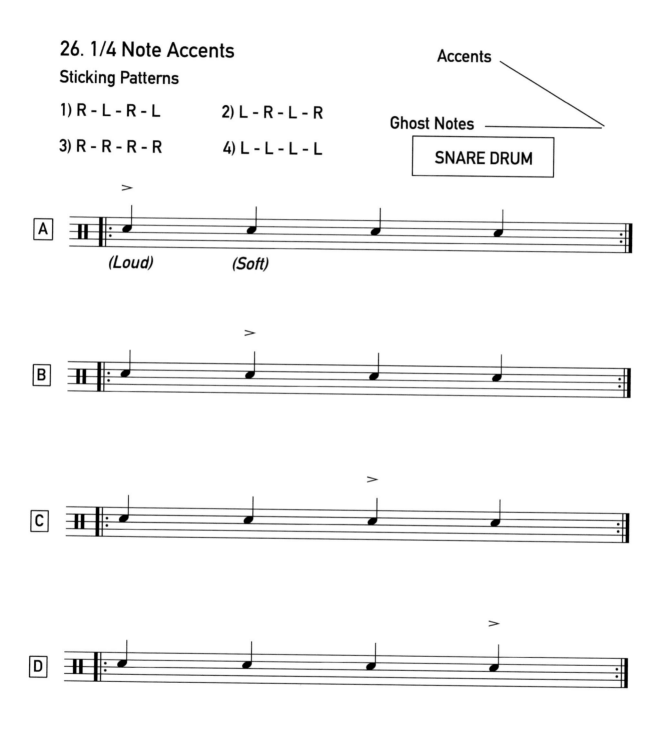

Stick Height:

1. Accents: Height of drumstick should be higher for a louder sound

2. Ghost Notes: Height of drumstick should be very low for a softer sound

3. Keep consistency of only two different volumes (Loud or Soft)

27. 1/8 Note Accents

Sticking Pattern

R - L - R - L - R - L - R - L

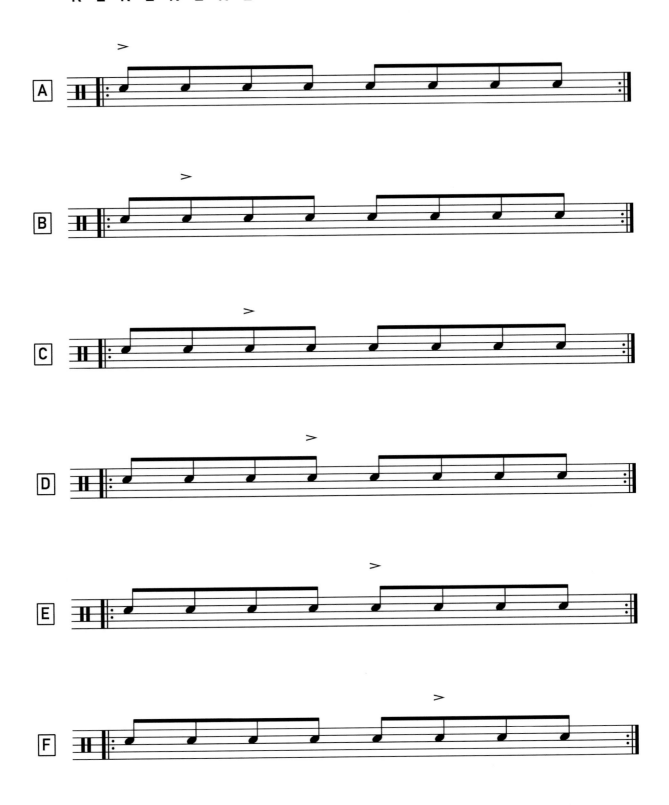

28

28. 1/16 Note Accents

Sticking Pattern
R – L – R – L

Combination Exercise

LESSON 5: (Fill-ins)

29. Full Bar Fill-ins   **30. Half Bar Fill-ins**   **31. 1 Beat Fill-ins**

29. Full Bar Fill-ins

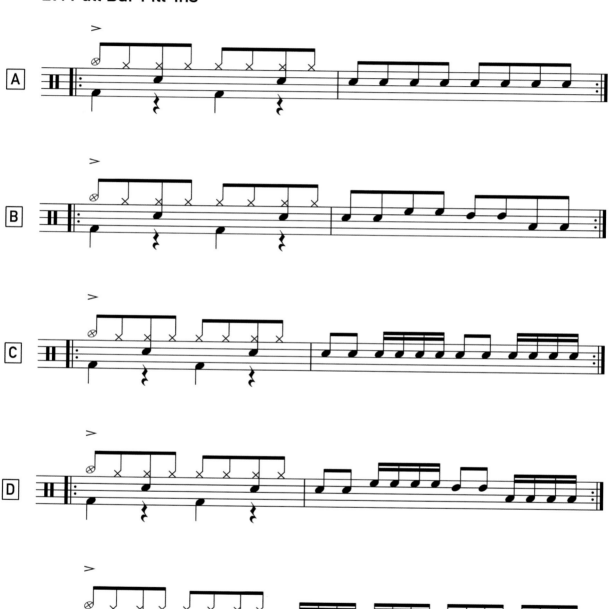

30. Half Bar Fill-ins

- Some sticking patterns need to be changed for the fill-ins (example: A3, B2)
Rule no.1 - keep the default sticking patterns
Rule no.2 - break the first rule only if you have to

31. One Beat Fill-ins

40

32. Rhythm + Fill-in

3+1

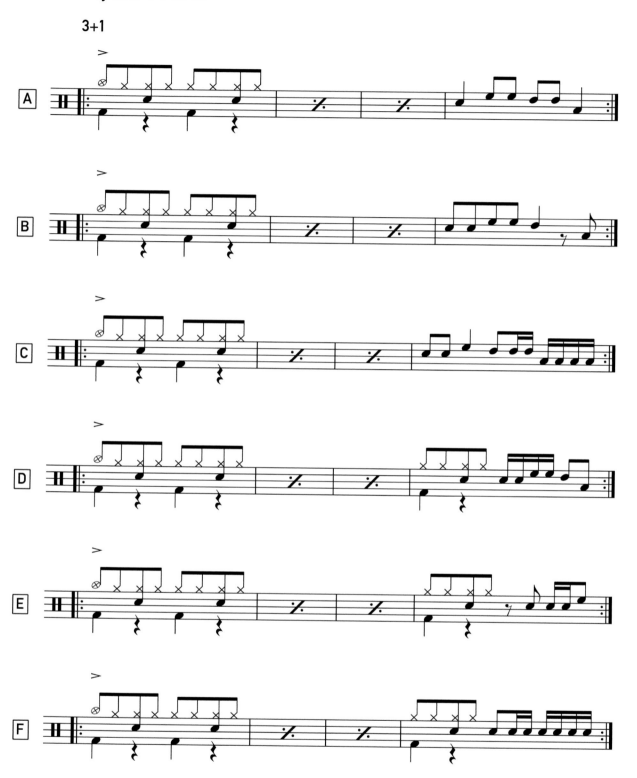

LESSON 6: (Triplets and Six-tuplets)

33. Triplets

COUNT: 1 e a   2 e a   3 e a   4 e a

34. 12/8 Rhythm

- Play these exercises replacing the Hi-Hat
with Ride Cymbal, Crash Cymbal, Floor Tom and Open Hi-Hat

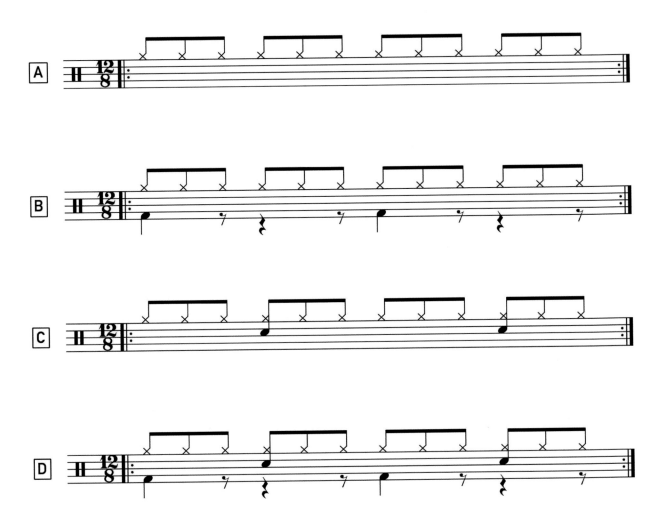

35. 12/8 Rhythm + Fill-in

36. Six-tuplets

A | RLRLRL ⟶

B | RLRLRL ⟶

C | RLRLRL ⟶

THE END

46

Printed in the United States
by Baker & Taylor Publisher Services